T0161248

Spiritual Secrets for Playing The Game of Life

Derived from

Florence Scovel Shinn's

The Game of Life & How to Play It

by Beverly A. Potter

Timeless Wisdom Series

RONIN
Berkeley, California

Spiritual Secrets for Playing the Game of Life

Copyright: 2011 by Beverly A. Potter
ISBN: 978-1-57951-132-6

Published by
Ronin Publishing, Inc.
PO Box 22900
Oakland, CA 94609
www.roninpub.com

Production:

Cover Design: Brian Groppe
www.BrianGroppe.com

Book Design: Beverly A. Potter

Library of Congress Card Number: 2011907301
Distributed to the book trade by PGW / Perseus
Printed in the United States

Derived from *The Game of Life & How to Play it* by Florence Scovel Shinn by Beverly A. Potter.

Table of Contents

Introduction

You may feel things happen to you and that life is a battle. Florence Scovel Shinn wisely advises, "Life is not a battle; life is a game." When you don't know the rules of the Game you make foolish moves and it feels like things happen to you, that you are "the effect"; actually you are "the cause". You are creating your life. Where you are today is the result of all of your past thoughts, feelings and actions. Where you are is the perfect place to be at this time in your life.

Laws govern the Game of Life, which when violated, make life a struggle. When you understand that life is actually a Spiritual Game, living becomes more joyful. In this little book Shinn shares wisdoms—Spiritual Secrets for playing the Game of Life— she gleaned from Infitite Intelligence and *The Bible*.

Life is a great game of boomerangs. What you put out comes back to you. This is an essential principle. When you put out negativity, negativity returns; whereas when you are positive, positive returns.

The power is in your Word. What you speak or think comes about. Listen to your thoughts and the words you say. Do they reflect what you want—or what you *don't* want. The reason you don't have what you want may be that you spend more time thinking about what you don't want than what you do want. If you obsess over what you don't have, you dwell in lack—so lack continues.

Through your spoken Word, you continually make laws for yourself. You define what can and will happen—or can't happen. You create your life through your Words, yet, it feels like your life is happening to you. You can change your life by changing your words.

Your ability to image—to create pictures—is key to playing the Game of Life. You can only receive what you can *see* yourself receiving. *You must believe* that what you want is yours by your Divine Right and that you will receive it.

Plenty is always on your path. But you cannot attract money if you despise it. You must feel and act opulent and give freely because giving opens the way to receiving. Giving shows faith—belief that you do have plenty. God—Infinite Intelligence—is your supply and your supply is inexhaustible.

In this comforting and inspiring little book you will learn Florence Shinn's wisdoms—her Spiritual Secrets. As you apply them, your life will begin to flow.

1

Spiritual Secret
Life is a Game

Life is a great game of giving and receiving.

Life feels like a battle—but it is not a battle; Life is a game of giving and receiving. Playing the Game of Life successfully takes knowledge of Spiritual Law. *The Bible* gives the rules of the Game with wonderful clearness.

Whatever you sow; you will also reap. If you plant corn, you will reap corn, not squash. If you plant squash, you will reap squash, not corn.

> *"Whatsoever a man soweth that shall he also reap."* (Galatians 6:7)

Seeds you sow today, good or bad, will bring a harvest of good or bad into your life—sooner or later.

> *"Whoever sows sparingly will also reap sparingly, and whoever sows generously will also reap generously."* (2 Corinthians 9:6)

2

Spiritual Secret

God's will be done.

~~~

**God's pattern—not your pattern—
is the command.**

The Bible deals with the Science of the Mind.
It tells how to release your Soul— subconscious mind—from bondage.

> *"A man's foes shall be they of his own household."* (Matthew 10:36)

Battles described in *The Bible* are pictures of
us waging war against mortal thoughts. Every
man is Jehoshaphat, and every man is David,
who slays Goliath—mortal thinking—with the
little white stone—faith

A student gave me an example of this when
she took an extended trip abroad one summer,
visiting many countries, where she was ignorant
of the languages. She called for guidance and
protection every minute and her affairs went
smoothly and miraculously. Her luggage was
never delayed nor lost! Accommodations were
always ready for her at the best hotels; and she
had perfect service wherever she went.

When she returned to New York, knowing the language, she felt God was no longer necessary, so she looked after her affairs in an ordinary manner. But everything went wrong, her trunks delayed, amid inharmony and confusion.

Form a habit of "practicing the Presence of God" every minute.

Sometimes you may hold back your demonstration of God's bounty through resistance or pointing the way. You may pin your faith to one channel only and dictate just the way you desire the manifestation of what you desire to come, which brings things to a standstill

An insignificant incident may be the turning point in your life. Robert Fulton, watching boiling water simmering in a tea kettle, saw a steamboat!

Like all Power, be it steam or electricity, Infinite Intelligence must have a nonresistant engine or instrument to work through.

You are

the instrument

though which

Infinite Intelligence works.

You are here to prove God and
"to bear witness to the Truth."

You prove God
by bringing
plenty out of lack
and justice out of injustice.

3

Spiritual Secret

The Law obeys you when you obey the Law.

∽◎∽◎∽

Obedience to the Law precedes manifesting.

The law of electricity must be obeyed before it becomes your servant. When handled ignorantly, it becomes a deadly foe. So, too, with Laws of Mind!

A woman envied an acquaintance's house where she often pictured herself living. In the course of time the acquaintance died and she moved into the house. Several years later, coming into the knowledge of Spiritual Law, she said to me: "Do you think I had anything to do with that man's death?"

I replied: "Yes, your desire was so strong, everything made way for it, but you paid your Karmic debt when your husband died soon after."

Desire is a tremendous force, and must be directed in the right channels, or chaos ensues. Feeling a great desire for the house, the woman should have said:

> "Infinite Intelligence, give me the right house, equally as charming as this house, which is mine by Divine Right."

4

Spiritual Secret

**Violation of the Law brings
about suffering.**

❦

**There is a penalty to be paid for
not using your ability.**

The more you know, the more your responsibility. A person with knowledge of Spiritual Law but who does not practice, suffers greatly. Boomerangs of hate, resentment and criticism, come back laden with sickness and sorrow when you violate the Law.

Many *Bible* passages are much clearer if you read the word "Lord" as "Law".

> *"The fear of the Lord (Law) is the beginning
> of wisdom."* (Psalm 111:10)

It is the *law* that takes vengeance, not God. God sees you as perfect, "created in his own image," (imagination) and given "power and dominion."

> *"Vengeance is mine, I will repay, saith
> the Lord (Law)."* (Romans 12:19)

5

Spiritual Secret

Trust the God within

∽≈⊙≈∽

When you relinquish personal will, you enable Infinite Intelligence to work through you.

Things go awry when you trust yourself over Infinite Intelligence. A boy who had an excellent knowledge of history, but was not sure of arithmetic asked me to "speak the Word" for his final exams. I told him to make the statement:

Confidence Affirmation

I am one with Infinite Intelligence. I know everything I should know on this subject.

After the exam, he said: "I spoke the Word for arithmetic, and passed with the highest honors, but not for history because I could depend on myself, but I got a very poor mark!"

"In all thy ways acknowledge him," (Proverbs 3:6)
nothing is too small or too great.

Like the boy, you may suffer a set-back when you are "too sure of yourself," which means you are trusting your personality and not the "God within."

"My way, not your way!"
is the command of Infinite Intelligence.

6

Spiritual Secret

There is a Divine Design
for your life.

~oe~~oe~

The Divine Design is your true destiny
—or destination

Your superconscious mind holds a perfect picture of your place in life that it flashes to you from the Infinite Intelligence, which is within you.

> *There is a place that you are to fill and no one else can fill, something you are to do, which no one else can do.* —Plato

Ignorant of your true destiny, you may strive for that which does not belong to you and that will bring failure and dissatisfaction if attained.

> *"Seek ye first the Kingdom of God and his righteousness; and all these things shall be added unto you."*
> (Matthew 6:33)

The Kingdom is the realm of right ideas
—the Divine Pattern.

Your destiny is a perfect idea in Divine Mind awaiting your recognition.

You may not have the faintest conception of what your destiny is, for there is, possibly, some marvelous talent, hidden deep within you.

Demand

Infinite Spirit, open the way for the Divine Design of my life to manifest; let the genius within me now be released; let me see clearly the perfect plan.

You may find great changes taking place in your life after making this demand, for nearly everyone has wandered far from the Divine Design.

Affirmation

I am fully equipped for the Divine Plan of my life.

The Law of Reincarnation

You will go through many births and deaths until you know the Truth, which sets you free from the cycle of death and rebirth. You are drawn back to the earth plane through unsatisfied desire, to pay your Karmic debts and to fulfill your destiny.

People born rich and healthy have had pictures in their subconscious mind, in their past lives, of health and riches; whereas the poor and sick have had pictures of disease and poverty. You manifests, on any plane, the sum total of your subconscious beliefs.

Parents should never force careers upon their children. With a knowledge of spiritual Truth, the Divine Plan could be spoken for, early in childhood, or prenatally.

Prenatal Demand

Let the God in this child have perfect expression; let the Divine Design of his mind, body and affairs be made manifest throughout this child's life, throughout eternity.

7

Spiritual Secret

Where you are is the perfect place to be at this time in your life.

Where you are today is the result of all of your past thoughts, feelings and actions.

When you accept yourself and your circumstances, you can release the hold of being stuck and move forward in your life. Embracing this Spiritual Secret enables you to regain power in your life.

You are on a path, although it may not be entirely clear where it is leading, but there is something crucial about the experiences you are having right now. Focus on the present. Give yourself permission to take stock in where you currently find yourself. What are you learning? What's important to you? What do you want to create?

Be happy now—today! Do not postpone being happy until you have succeeded or achieved what you believe will bring you happiness.

Start Now! Give yourself credit for all your past achievements while looking forward to an even better future.

Happiness can only

be experienced

in the

NOW.

8

Spiritual Secret

Imaging is key to winning at the Game of Life.

What you image manifests in your affairs.

Picture good and good comes to you, bringing righteous desires of your heart—health, wealth, love, friends, actualization, your highest ideals.

> *"Keep thy heart (or imagination) with all diligence,*
> *for out of it are the issues of life."* (Proverbs. 4:23)

Imagination is the scissors of your mind cutting day-by-day the pictures you create. Sooner or later you meet your creations.

You must understand the workings of your mind to train your imaging-ability.

Know thyself
—Socrates

Three Departments of Mind
—the Subconscious, Conscious and Superconscious.

The *subconscious mind* is simply power, without direction—like steam or electricity. It has no power of induction. It does not initiate, but does as it is directed. Whatever you image or picture clearly is impressed upon your subconscious mind and carried out in minutest detail.

The *conscious or reasoning mind* is the intellect. It judges, questions and challenges, finds lack and limitation, is skeptical, and fosters doubts and fear. It impresses the subconscious.

The *superconscious mind* is the God within you. Here is where faith finds it's support and strength. Superconscious mind is a well-within from which intuition, your unerring guide, receives it's knowing from Infinite Intelligence, which it sends to you through the conscious mind in images or picture-flashes and hunches.

Imaging

*V*isualizing is a mental process governed by the reasoning or conscious mind; *imaging or visioning* is a spiritual process of creating pictures governed by intuition, or the superconscious mind. Do not visualize or force a mental picture, which is using your conscious mind.

Train your conscious mind *to receive* flashes of inspiration from your intuition to help find definite leads to working out the "Divine Picture". When you can say, "I desire only that which God desires for me," false desires fade from the consciousness, and a new set of blue-prints are given to you, by the Master Architect, the God within.

God's plan for you transcends the limitations of your reasoning mind and is always the Square of Life, containing health, wealth, love and perfect self-expression.

Hunches and flashes come from intuition.

As you open conscious mind to receiving flashes of inspiration, you will begin to see yourself making some great accomplishment. Hold this picture or vision, without wavering.

9

Spiritual Secret

**You can only receive what
you 'see' yourself receiving.**

◈

**Every good and perfect gift is already yours
awaiting your recognition.**

The children of Israel were told that they
could have all the land they could see. This
is true for each of us. You can only have the land
within your mental vision.

> *"Before ye call I shall answer."*
> (Isaiah 65:24)

Jesus' clear vision pierced the world of matter. He
saw the fourth dimensional world—things as they
really are, perfect and complete in Divine Mind.

> *"Say not ye, there are yet four months and then
> cometh the harvest? Behold, I say unto you, lift up
> your eyes and look on the fields; for they are ripe
> already to harvest."* (John 4:35)

Every great work, every big accomplishment
has been brought into manifestation through *holding to a Vision.* Often just before the big achievement, comes apparent failure and discouragement.

What you feel deeply, good or bad, is out-pictured by your subconscious mind. The sick man has pictured sickness, the poor man, poverty, the rich man, wealth.

*You are bound
by the expectancies
of your subconscious.*

You may be limiting yourself in your demands. For example: A student made the demand for six hundred dollars by a certain date. He did receive it, but heard afterwards, that he came very near receiving a thousand dollars, but he was given just six hundred, as the result of his spoken Word.

*"The desert shall rejoice and
blossom as the rose."* (Isaiah 35:1)

Rejoicing while yet in the desert—state of lack—opens the way for release. In making demands, *declare that you have already received it* —and rejoice.

*Enlarge your expectancies
to receive in a larger way.*

10

Spiritual Secret

**Hold to the vision of your
journey's end**

~~~~~

**Demand the manifestation of that which
you have *already* received.**

Be it perfect health, love, supply, self-expression, home or friends, these are finished and
perfect ideas registered in Divine Mind—your
superconscious mind.

You must <u>picture</u> your demand,

before it can manifest.

It must come through you,
not to you.

Make a Demonstration

A demonstration is a revelation of God's supply, which is inexhaustible.

Speak the Word, then do not do anything until you get a definite lead. Demand the lead, saying:

> "Infinite spirit, reveal to me the way, let me know if there is anything for me to do."

Leads that point the way come through intuition—a hunch, perhaps a chance remark from someone, or a passage in a book. Answers can be quite startling in their exactness.

A woman who desired a large sum of money spoke the Word: "Infinite Spirit, open the way for my immediate supply, let all that is mine by Divine Right now reach me, in great avalanches of abundance." She added: "Give me a definite lead, let me know if there is anything for me to do."

A thought came quickly, "Give a certain friend—who had helped her spiritually—a hundred dollars." She told her friend, who said, "Wait and get another lead, before giving it." So she waited, and that day met a woman who said to her, "I gave someone a dollar today; it was just as much for me, as it would be for you to give someone a hundred."

It was an unmistakable lead, so she knew she was right in giving the hundred dollars. It was a gift that proved a great investment, for shortly after that, a large sum of money came to her in a remarkable way.

Faith must precede the demonstration.
Faith holds your Vision steady.

Faith, your unwavering belief in God's supply, dissolves and dissipates the adverse pictures and holds your Vision steady.

> *"Faith is the substance of things hoped for, the evidence of things not seen..."* (Hebrew 11:1)

Your supply is unfailing when fully trusted.

11

Spiritual Secret

**Demand definite leads and the way
will be made easy and successful.**

**Your highest demand is for
the Divine Design of your life.**

You come into the world financed by God, the supply needed for your perfect self-Expression will be at hand.

You may have several talents and wonder how to know which one to choose?" Demand to be shown definitely.

Demand for a Lead

Infinite Spirit, give me a definite lead, reveal
to me my perfect self-Expression, show me
which talent I am to make use of now.

I have known people to suddenly enter a new line of work, and be fully equipped, with little or no training. Repeat the demand and be fearless in grasping opportunities.

*Be spiritually alert,
take advantage of every opportunity.*

Look for "Signs of Land"

Before Columbus reached America, he saw birds and twigs, which showed him land was near. So it is with a demonstration; but often the student mistakes it for the demonstration itself, and is disappointed.

A woman had "spoken the Word" for a set of dishes. Not long afterwards a friend gave her a dish that was old and cracked. She complained, "Well, I asked for a set of dishes, and all I got was a cracked plate."

I replied, "The plate was only a sign of land. It shows dishes are coming—look upon it as birds and seaweed, "and not long afterwards the dishes came.

Leads come in unexpected ways.

One day, I was taking a walk and I felt a urge to go to a certain bakery, a block away. My reasoning mind resisted, "There is nothing there that you want." However, I had learned not to reason when presented with a "sense" or hunch, so I went to the bakery, looked, but there was nothing I wanted, however coming out I encountered a woman who was in need of the help I could give her.

When you *demand* of Infinite Intelligence, be ready for surprises.

Awoman was resentful because she lost five thousand dollars she'd loaned to a relative who died without leaving mention of it in her will. She decided to collect her money from the Bank of the Universe. But first she had to forgive her relative, because resentment and unforgiveness close the doors of this wonderful bank.

The woman spoke these words, "I deny loss, there is no loss in Divine Mind, therefore, I cannot lose the five thousand dollars, which belong to me by Divine Right." As one door shuts another door opens.

The apartment house where she lived was for sale. A clause in her lease stated that if the building was sold, the tenants would be required to move out within ninety days.

Unexpectedly, the landlord broke the leases and raised the rent. Again, injustice was on her pathway, but this time she was undisturbed. She blessed the landlord, and said this affirmation:

Affirmation
As the rent has been raised,
it means that I'll be that much richer,
for God is my supply.

New leases were made out for the advanced rent, but by some Divine mistake, the ninety days clause had been forgotten. Soon after, the landlord had an opportunity to sell the building. Because of the mistake in the new leases, the tenants were entitled to possession for another year.

The realtor offered the tenants a thousand dollars each to vacate. Several families moved; three remained, including the woman. A month later the realtor came back with a new offer: "Will you break your lease for the sum of three thousand dollars?" It flashed upon her, "Here comes the five thousand dollars." Remembering saying to other tenants, "We will all act together if anything more is said about leaving." So her lead was to consult her friends.

These friends said, "Well, if they have offered you three thousand they will certainly give five thousand." So she received a check for five thousand dollars for giving up the apartment. It was certainly a remarkable working of the Law, and the apparent injustice was merely opening the way for her demonstration.

Everything may seem to be going wrong, when in reality, it is going right

12

Spiritual Secret

**You cannot force the external
to be what you are not.**

❦

**If you desire riches, you must first
be rich in consciousness.**

A woman whose home was messy because she did not take much interest in her household affairs asked me for treatment for prosperity. I explained, "If you wish to be rich, you must be orderly. All men with great wealth are orderly—order is Heaven's first Law." I added, "You will never become rich with a burnt match in the pin-cushion."

She had a good sense of humor and commenced immediately to put her house in order, rearranging furniture, straightening out bureau drawers, cleaning rugs. Shortly after she received a big financial gift from a relative. Thereafter, she became made over, being ever watchful of the external and expecting prosperity, knowing God is her supply.

Affirmation
My supply is inexhaustible.

13

Spiritual Secret

A silent listener—your subconscious mind—is always by your side.

The subconscious is your faithful servant but you must give it the right orders.

Every thought, every word is impressed upon your subconscious and carried out in amazing detail. Like a singer making a recording, every note and tone is registered. If the singer coughs or hesitates, it is registered. Break the old bad records in your subconscious mind, make new and beautiful records of your life to replace the unhappy, dark ones. Speak the Affirmation with power and conviction.

Affirmation

I now smash and demolish—by my spoken Word—every untrue record in my subconscious mind. They shall return to the dustheap of their native nothingness, for they came from my own vain imaginings. I now make my perfect records through the God within—records of Health, Wealth, Love and perfect self-Expression.

This is the Square of Life.

The Square of Life
is Health, Wealth, Love
and perfect self-Expression,
which brings perfect happiness
—the Game completed.

14

Spiritual Secret

**Your work is in making
yourself believe.**

~~~~~~

Affirming establishes belief in the subconscious.

You would not have to make an affirmation more than once if you had perfect faith! This is easy enough to state in the abstract, but a little more difficult when confronted with a problem.

A woman needed to demonstrate a large sum of money within a stated time. She knew she must do something to get a realization to demand a lead. She was walking through a department store and felt a "pull" towards a beautiful pink enamel paper cutter. The thought came. "I haven't a paper cutter to open letters containing large cheques."

She bought the paper cutter that her reasoning mind called extravagant. Holding it in her hand, she had a flash of a picture of herself opening an envelope with a large cheque. A few weeks later, she received the money. The pink paper cutter was her bridge of active faith.

"Be ye transformed by the renewing of your mind."
(Romans 12:2)

Following a lead shows active faith.

15

Spiritual Secret

**"Making-believe" impresses
the subconscious.**

Fake it and you will make it.

Children love to "make believe". When you
act as if you can do something, you discover
you are doing it!

*"Except ye be converted, and become as little chil-
dren, ye shall not enter the Kingdom of Heaven."*
(Matthew 18:3)

I knew an impoverished woman, but no one
could make her feel poor. Rich friends urged
her to not spend, but save. Regardless of their
admonitions, she would spend all her earnings
on a hat, or buy someone a gift, which put her
in a rapturous state of mind. Her thoughts were
always centered on beautiful clothes and "rings
and things," but without envying others.

Her world was wondrous, where only riches
were real to her. Before long she married a rich
man, and the rings and things became visible.
I don't know if the man was her "Divine Selection," but opulence had to manifest in her life, as
she had imaged only opulence.

16

Spiritual Secret

Affirmations must be convincing and satisfying to your subconscious

Singing affirmations that rhyme is powerful.

Music has a fourth dimensional quality that makes wonderful things seem possible and easy to accomplishment. It can move your subconscious into perfect harmony, releasing your image-ability. Singing an affirmation, while dancing, increases its power for sinking into the subconscious.

A business man changed the word "work" to "business" and repeated, "I have a wonderful business, in a wonderful way, and I give wonderful service for wonderful pay." That afternoon he made an unexpected forty-one thousand dollar deal.

Good Work Affirmation
I have wonderful work,
in a wonderful way,
I give wonderful service,
for wonderful pay!

17

Spiritual Secret

Words are the instrument with which you play the Game of Life.

You change your conditions by changing your words.

Words and thoughts—self-talk—are ever molding your body and affairs. Through your spoken Word you can release all that belongs to you by Divine Right. But you must have perfect faith.

> *"By your words ye are justified and by your words ye are condemned."*
> (Matthew 12:37)

Words can change a situation of lack into one of plenty.

Plenty is always on your path. Plenty is manifested through desire, faith and the spoken Word.

Power

is in your Word.

18

Spiritual Secret

**Your subconscious mind creates
what you tell it to bring forth.**

⌇⌇

**With every word you speak you improve or
destroy your health, relationships, finances.**

Every sound you utter sends out an energy wave—a prayer—that aids in creating the world you experience.

> *"All things whatsoever ye ask in
> prayer, believing, ye shall receive."*
> (Matthew 21:22)

Before you can manifest desires, you must decide what you want and express that desire in words. When you tell your subconscious mind that life provides opportunities, you will have opportunities; tell it that you never get what you want and disappointment will prevail.

Choose one thing you desire and write it down in a short sentence. Write in the present tense as if it were already so. Be specific. If your desire is financial avoid, generalities like, "I am rich." Instead, be specific, "I have a monthly net income of $10,000" or "I receive a windfall of $250,000" or "I sell my novel for $50K advance.

Through your spoken Word, you continually make laws for yourself.

You become careful in conversation when you know the power of the Word.

A man said, "I always miss the bus. It invariably pulls out just as I arrive." His daughter said: "I always catch the bus. It's sure to come just as I get there." They each had made a separate law for themselves, one of failure, one of success. This is the psychology of superstition.

A man who had had great success in business was suddenly hit with loses. Instead of making affirmations and looking to God for success and prosperity, he bought a "lucky charm." But things just got worse because he put his trust in lucky charms instead of God.

The horseshoe or rabbit's foot contains no power, but our spoken Word and belief that it will bring good luck creates expectancy in the subconscious mind, which attracts a "lucky" or "unlucky" situation.

This does not mean you should throw away a lucky charm, rather recognize that the power behind the charm is the one and only power—God. The object simply gives a feeling of expectancy.

A despairing friend picked up a horseshoe she found along the street and was filled with joy and hope because she believed God had sent her the horseshoe to keep up her courage.

Her hope became faith and she ultimately made a wonderful recovery from her depression. The difference between her and the man with the lucky charm is that the man put his faith in the charm alone, while the woman recognized that God was the power behind the horseshoe.

In my case, it took a long while to get out of a belief that a certain thing brought disappointment. If the thing happened, disappointment invariably followed. I found the only way I could make a change in my subconscious was by speaking the affirmation: "There is only one power—God. Therefore, there are no disappointments. This thing means a happy surprise." I noticed a change at once, and happy surprises commenced coming my way.

Most of us don't know how to use the power that we have.

By not manifesting properly or losing faith when your desire doesn't happen quickly enough you may sabotage the manifesting by allowing your thoughts to focus on what you don't have, what you don't see, and what you don't want.

You continuously
manifest your life through
your thoughts and your images.

19

Spiritual Secret
What you voice, you attract.

∿◦――◦∿

Curses, like chickens, come home to roost.

You are always "pulling the strings" yourself, though you don't know it. Owing to the vibratory power of words, whatever you voice, you attract. People who continually speak of disease, invariably attract it.

> *"Death and Life are in the power of the tongue."* (Proverb 18:21)

What you say of others will be said of you, and what you wish for another, you wish for yourself. If you wish someone "bad luck," you will attract bad luck yourself. If you wish someone success, you are wishing yourself success.

Use your Words to heal, bless and prosper.

20

Spiritual Secret

Be careful to decree that only the Divine Idea be made manifest

~~~~

Be careful of idle words that can decree failure or misfortune.

What is manifest in your life is released through your recognition, or spoken Word. So it is of the utmost importance to word your demands correctly—so that only the Divine Idea be manifest.

> *"Thou shalt also decree a thing, and it shall be established unto thee."* (Job 22:28)

If you desire a home, friend, position or other good thing, make the demand for the "Divine Selection."

Demand for Divine Selection

Infinite Spirit, open the way for my right home, my right friend, my right position. I give thanks that it now manifests under grace in a perfect way.

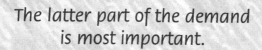

*The latter part of the demand
is most important.*

A woman demanded a thousand dollars. Soon after her daughter was injured and they received a thousand dollars indemnity, but the money did not come in a "perfect way." The demand should have been worded in this way:

> "Infinite Spirit, I give thanks that the one thousand dollars, which is mine by Divine Right, is now released, and reaches me under grace, in a perfect way."

A woman in need said an affirmation for work. She received a great deal of work, but was not paid anything. She needed to add, "wonderful service for wonderful pay.

*Affirmations must be carefully worded
to completely cover the need.*

Spiritual Secret
**Through the spoken Word, failure
can be transmuted into success.**

❧❦

A feeling of opulence must precede
its manifestation.

A metaphysician gave me a wonderful secret for winning in the Game of Life. "At one time in my life," he said, "I baptized children, and of course, they had many names. Now I no longer baptize children; I baptize events, but I give every event the same name. If I have a failure I baptize it success, in the name of the Father, and of the Son, and of the Holy Ghost!"

A woman in need of money had a colleague who made her feel impoverish because he talked lack and limitation, which she would catch. She knew in order to demonstrate her supply, she must first feel that she had already received.

She realized she was resisting the situation by seeing two powers instead of one. She reminded herself that all people are God in manifestation, awaiting the opportunity given by us, to serve the Divine Plan of our lives. So she blessed the man and baptized the situation "Success"!

She affirmed, "As there is only one power, God. This man is here for my good and my prosperity"—just what he did not seem to be there for. Never the less she spoke the words to transmute failure into success.

A short while later the negative man introduced her to a woman who became a client and paid her several thousand dollars. Soon after the man moved to a distant city, fading harmoniously from her life.

Affirmation
Every person is a golden
link in the chain of my good.

22

Spiritual Secret

**Begin the day with
the right Words.**

**Make an affirmation immediately
upon waking.**

Make it a habit to say a positive affirmation upon waking each morning, and you will see wonders and miracles come into your life.

Morning Affirmation
Thy will be done this day!
Today is a day of completion;
I give thanks for this perfect day,
miracle shall follow miracle
and wonders shall never cease.

23

Spiritual Secret

Intuition is your unerring guide.

⮜⮞

**Intuition means, in-tuition,
or to be taught from within**

A woman with just eight dollars in the world asked for a "treatment" for prosperity. "Good," I said, "we'll bless the eight dollars and multiply them as Jesus multiplied the loaves and fishes," for He taught that we all have the power to bless and to multiply, to heal and to prosper.

"What shall I do next?" she asked. "Follow your intuition," I replied. "Have you a 'hunch' to do something, or to go somewhere?"

"I have a 'hunch' to go home," she replied. Her home life had been one of lack and limitation. Her reasoning mind argued: "Stay in New York and make money here." Supporting her intuition, I said, "Never ignore a hunch— Go home." I spoke the following Words and told her to repeat the prayer continually:

> Infinite Spirit open the way for great abundance
> for this woman. She is an irresistible magnet for
> all that belongs to her by Divine Right.

She went home, where she linked up with an old family friend through whom she received thousands of dollars in a most miraculous way.

Don't look to the psychic plane for guidance.

The psychic plane is the plane of many minds and not the "The One Mind."

As you open your mind to subjectivity, you become a target for destructive forces. The psychic plane is the result of your mortal thought, and is on the "plane of opposites." You may receive either good or bad messages.

The science of numbers and the reading of horoscopes, keep you on the mental or mortal plane, for they deal only with the Karmic path.

24

Spiritual Secret

**Intuition simply points
the way.**

∾≀∽∾≀∽

Intuition doesn't explain or follow logic.

In class, one day, I was treating that they would each receive a definite lead. A woman came to me afterwards, and said: "While you were treating, I got the hunch to take my furniture out of storage and get an apartment."

The woman had come to be treated for health. I told her I knew in getting a home of her own, her health would improve, and I added, "I believe your trouble, which is a congestion, has come from having things stored away. Congestion of things causes congestion in the body. You have violated the Law of Use, and your body is paying the penalty."

I gave thanks that "Divine Order was established in her mind, body and affairs."

Affirmation for Guidance

I am divinely sensitive to my intuitive leads,
and give instant obedience to Thy will.

Prayer
is command and demand,
praise and thanksgiving.

"Ask and ye shall receive."
(Philippians 4:6)

"And all things, whatever you shall ask in prayer, believing, you shall receive." (Mathew 21:22)

Demand only that which is yours by Divine Right.

The Lord's Prayer

begins with a command and demand:

*"Give us this day our daily bread,
and forgive us our debts
as we forgive our debtors,"*

and ends in praise,

*"For thine is the Kingdom and
the Power and the Glory, forever.*

—Amen."

25

Spiritual Secret

You must make the first move.

❦❧

You must demand.

Every desire—uttered or unexpressed—is a demand. God—Infinite Intelligence—is ready to carry out your smallest or greatest demands.

> *"Concerning the works of my hands, command ye me."* (Isaiah 45:11)

A desire can be suddenly fulfilled as happened to me one Easter. Having seen a beautiful rose-tree in the florists' windows, I wished I would receive one, and for an instant saw it mentally being carried in my door. Easter came, and with it a beautiful rose-tree. When I thanked my friend for her thoughtfulness because it was just what I had wanted, she replied, "I didn't send you a rose-tree, I sent you lilies!" My wish for a rose-tree started the Law in action so the man had mixed the order. *I had asked for a rose-tree.*

> *Ask, and it shall be given you, seek, and ye shall find, knock, and it shall be opened unto you."* (Matthew 7:7)

26

~~~~~

Spiritual Secret

Do not hesitate to ask for help.

∽◦᠗◦᠗◦∽

You cannot fail, if some one person sees you as successful.

When we get too close to our affairs we become doubtful and fearful. Whereas friends and "healers" see clearly your success, health, or prosperity because they are not close to the situation.

"If two of you shall agree on earth as touching anything that they shall ask, it shall be done for them of my Father which is in heaven." (Matthew 18:19)

It was imperative for a man to raise fifty-thousand dollars. The time limit was almost up, when he came to me in despair. No one wanted to invest and the bank had refused a loan. I replied: "I suppose you lost your temper at the bank, therefore your power. You can control any situation when you control yourself."

"Go back to the bank," I directed, "and I will treat." My treatment was:

You are identified in love with the spirit of everyone connected with the bank. Let the Divine Idea come out of this situation.

He replied, "Woman, you are talking about an impossibility. Tomorrow is Saturday; the bank closes at twelve, and my train won't get me there until ten. My time limit is up tomorrow, and anyway they won't do it. It's too late."

I replied, "God doesn't need any time and is never too late. With Him all things are possible." I added, "I don't know anything about business, but I know all about God." He replied: "It all sounds fine when I sit here listening to you, but when I go out it's terrible."

A letter came the following week. It read: "You were right. I raised the money, and will never again doubt the Truth of all that you told me."

When I saw him next, I asked, "What happened? You evidently had plenty of time, after all." He replied, "My train was late, and I got there just fifteen minutes to twelve. I walked into the bank quietly and said, 'I have come for the loan,' and they gave it to me without a question."

It was the last fifteen minutes of the time allotted to him and Infinite Spirit was not too late. In this instance the man could never have demonstrated alone. He needed someone to help him hold to the Vision. This is what we can do for one another.

Many a great man owes his success to a wife, or sister, or a friend who "believed in him" and held without wavering to the perfect vision!

27

Spiritual Secret

As the within, so the without.

⚬⚬⚬⚬

**External inharmony reflects
mental inharmony.**

The Universe rearranges itself to reflect your reality. Inharmony on the external, indicates mental inharmony. If you feel secure, loved, safe and happy inside, you will have a secure, safe and happy life surrounded by people who love you.

If you are angry inside, even when it's so deeply buried you are unaware of it, angry people will fill your life to mirror your denied anger back to you.

If you have a deep sense of abandonment people will leave you, withdraw emotionally, or even die. If you constantly beat yourself up with self-criticism, you will attract people who will put you down and may even physically hurt you.

*Your life mirrors your deep,
often unconscious, inner feelings.*

One of my students had a habit of lying. I told her it was a failure method and if she lied, she would be lied to. "I don't care," she defended, "I can't possibly get along without lying."

One day she was speaking on the phone to a man she was in love with, she turned to me and whispered, "I don't trust him, I know he's lying to me." "Well, you lie yourself," I reminded, "so someone has to lie to you, and you may be sure it will be just the person you want the truth from."

Some time after that, I saw her, and she said, "I'm cured of lying." "What cured you?" I questioned. She replied, "My roommate lies worse than I did!"

Life is a mirror.

28

Spiritual Secret

**Every disease has a
mental correspondence.**

❧❧❧

**Destructive thinking, hoarding, hating, fearing,
condemning encourage disease.**

You might receive instantaneous healing
through the realization of your body being
a perfect idea in Divine Mind, and, therefore,
whole and perfect, but if you continue your negative thinking, the disease will return because your
subconscious out-pictures what you image.

Metaphysicians know that all disease has a
mental correspondence, and in order to heal the
body you must first "heal the soul." Your Soul—
subconscious mind—must be washed whiter
than snow, for permanent healing.

You may wonder why a little child attracts
illness? Children are sensitive and receptive to
thoughts about them and often out-picture their
parents' fears. Mothers can unconsciously attract illness and disaster by continually holding
mental pictures of catastrophe, while watching
for symptoms.

29

Spiritual Secret

**Give a perfect love and you will
receive a perfect love.**

**Love is the strongest magnet force
in the universe.**

L ove seems almost a lost art. Real love is
selfless and free from fear. Real love pours
itself out upon the object of its affection, without
demanding any return. Its joy is in the joy of ,
unselfish love draws to itself its own; it does not
need to seek or demand.

> *"A new commandment I give unto you,
> that ye love one another."* (John 13:34)

Scarcely anyone has the faintest conception
of real love. We are selfish, tyrannical or fearful
in our affections, thereby losing the thing we
love.

Jealousy is the worst enemy of love, for the
imagination runs riot, seeing the loved one attracted to another, and invariably these fears
objectify if they are not neutralized.

30

Spiritual Secret

Love melts a cold heart.

∽◎∽◎∽

**Love and goodwill are invaluable in
business and friendship.**

A woman came to me, complaining of her employer, who was cold and critical and didn't want her in the position.

> *"There is peace on earth for him who sends
> goodwill to man!"* (Hebrews 12:14)

"Well," I replied, "Salute the Divinity in the woman and send her love." She said "I can't; she's a marble woman."

I answered, "You remember the story of the sculptor who asked for a certain piece of marble. He was asked why he wanted it, and he replied, 'because there is an angel in the marble,' and out of it he produced a wonderful work of art."

She said, "Very well, I'll try it." A week later she came back and said, "I did what you told me to, and now the woman is very kind, and took me for a ride in her new car."

> *"Love is the fulfilling of the Law."* (Romans 13:10)

A student asked me, month after month, to clean her consciousness of resentment. After a while, she arrived at the point where she resented only one woman, but that one woman kept her busy. Little by little she became poised and harmonious, and one day, all her resentment was wiped out.

She came in radiant, and exclaimed "You can't understand how I feel! The woman said something to me and instead of being furious I was loving and kind, and she apologized and was perfectly lovely to me. No one can understand the marvelous lightness I feel within!"

Goodwill produces an aura of protection about the one who sends it.

Don't avoid the people you fear. Instead meet them cheerfully, and they will either prove "golden links in the chain of one's good," or disappear harmoniously from your pathway.

Spiritual Secret
God is Love; God is Supply

❦❧

**Follow the path of love and
all things are added.**

Follow the path of selfishness and greed, and your supply vanishes, or you are separated from it.

I knew a very rich woman, who hoarded her income. She rarely gave anything away, but bought and bought and bought things for herself.

She was very fond of necklaces, and a friend once asked her how many she possessed. She replied, "Sixty-seven." She bought them and put them away, carefully wrapped in tissue paper. Had she used the necklaces it would have been quite legitimate, but she was violating "the Law of Use." Her closets were filled with clothes she never wore. Her jewel box filled jewels she never wore.

The woman's arms gradually became paralyzed from holding on to things, and eventually she was considered incapable of looking after her affairs and her wealth was handed over to others to manage.

Affirmations for Right Conditions

Divine Love now dissolves and dissipates
every wrong condition in
my mind, body and affairs.

Every plan my Father in heaven has not planned,
shall be dissolved and dissipated, and the Divine
Idea now comes to pass.

Only that which is true of God is true of me, for I
and the Father are ONE.

Divine Love is the most powerful chemical
in the universe, and dissolves everything
which is not of itself!

32

Spiritual Secret
**Disease is caused by
a mind not at ease.**

In the wake of unforgiveness are endless ills.

Holding grievances hardens arteries and liver, and affects eyesight. Constant criticism produces rheumatism, as critical inharmonious thoughts cause unnatural deposits in the blood that settle in the joints.

A woman told me she was ill from having eaten a poisoned oyster. I replied, "Oh, no, the oyster was harmless, you poisoned the oyster. Who's the matter with you?" She answered, "Oh about nineteen people." She had quarreled with nineteen people and had become so inharmonious that she attracted the wrong oyster.

If you have a pain in the neck, ask yourself, "Who am I allowing to be a pain in the neck?" If you have a pain in the heart, ask, "Who am I allowing to hurt me?" If you have indigestion, ask, "What is it that I can't stomach?" If you have an ache, ask, "Who or what am I aching for?"

*Instead of, "What's the matter with you?"
ask, "Who's the matter with you?"*

Affirmations for Health

Divine Love floods my consciousness
with health, and every cell in my body
is filled with light.

For Eyesight

My eyes are God's eyes,
I see with the eyes of spirit.
I see clearly the open way;
there are no obstacles on my pathway.
I see clearly the perfect plan.

For Hearing

My ears are God's ears,
I hear with the ears of spirit.
I am nonresistant and am willing to be led.
I hear glad tidings of great joy.

33

Spiritual Secret

Forgiveness purifies you.

～⚬～⚬～

**You cannot be forgiven until you
first forgive.**

As long as you harbor hate, anger, intolerance, criticism towards others you cannot purify yourself. It is in forgiving others that you forgive yourself.

When you hold on to anger and resentment, you build a negative dam of energy that stops good from coming to your life.

Forgiveness doesn't mean the other person was correct in their actions that hurt you. Forgiveness breaks a bond of negativity between you and the other person. When you forgive, the energy that has bonded you to another in a negative stagnant way is immediately released to come into your life in a positive manner, which makes way for the energies to work towards your desires and highest good.

Forgiving is one of the most loving and positive things you can do for yourself —and others.

Sickness and unhappiness come from violations of the Law of Love.

An actress, with an unattractive skin disease that doctors said was incurable, feared she would be forced to give up acting. So she was elated when she procured a good engagement, which was a great "hit" on opening night and received rave reviews. But she was dismissed the next day because of a meddling jealous men in the cast. The actress felt the hatred and resentment taking possession of her and cried out, "Oh God don't let me hate that man."

She said, "I came into a very deep silence and was at peace with myself, with the man, and with the whole world. I continued this for the next two nights, and on the third day I found that the skin disease was completely healed."

In asking for love, or goodwill, the actress had fulfilled the Law—for love is the fulfilling of the Law—and the skin disease, which came from subconscious resentment, was wiped out.

"Love one another,"
(John 13:34)

The Law of Forgiveness

The Law of Grace, or forgiveness, is a higher law than the Law of Karma and transcends it. The Law of Grace free us from the Law of Cause and Effect—consequences.

Christianity is founded upon the Law of Forgiveness. Jesus redeemed you from the curse of the Karmic law. The God within is your Redeemer and provides Salvation from all inharmonious conditions.

Picture the person you wish to forgive in your mind and state a positive affirmation of forgiveness.

Forgiveness Affirmation

I forgive you completely and freely,
I free you and let you go. What happened
between us is finished forever. I wish the
best for you, I wish for you your highest good,
and I hold you in the light. I am free and you are free,
and all is well between us from now on.
Peace be with you.

—Catharine Ponder
The Dynamic Laws of Prosperity

A woman who had received a counterfeit twenty-dollar bill at the bank lamented, "The people at the bank will never acknowledge their mistake." I replied, "Let us analyze the situation and find out why you attracted it." She thought a few moments: "I know it, I sent a friend a lot of stage-money, just for a joke." So the Law had sent her some stage-money, for it doesn't know anything about jokes. I said, "Now call on the Law of Forgiveness to neutralize the situation."

So I said: "Infinite Spirit, we call on the Law of Forgiveness and give thanks that she is under grace and not under Law, and cannot lose this twenty dollars, which is hers by Divine Right."

"Now go back to the bank and tell them, fearlessly, that it was given you there by mistake," I instructed. She obeyed, and to her surprise, they apologized and, treating her most courteously, gave her another bill.

"Under grace, and not under law."
(Romans 6:14)

34

Spiritual Secret

**Kindness in the present can
neutralize a wrong in the past**

∽∾∽∾∽

The mortal mind hangs onto regrets.

We are sometimes filled with remorse for having done someone an unkindness, perhaps years ago. Sorrow, regret, and remorse tear down the cells of the body, and poison the atmosphere of the self.

> *"This one thing I do, forgetting those things which are behind and reaching forth unto those things where are before."* (Philippians 3:13)

A woman in deep sorrow said, "Treat me to be happy and joyous, for my sorrow makes me so irritable with the members of my family that I keep making more Karma."

I denied all belief in loss and separation, and affirmed that God was the woman's joy, love and peace.

The woman gained her poise at once, but sent word by her son, not to treat any longer, because she was "so happy, it wasn't respectable."

Spiritual Secret
Fear is your enemy.

**Doubt and fear is all that stand between you
and every desire of your heart.**

One of the greatest messages in the scriptures
is that God is your inexhaustible and unfailing supply and that you can release, through
your spoken Word, all that belongs to you by
Divine Right. But *you must have perfect faith in
your spoken Word.*

A successful man erased fear from his consciousness after reading a sign: "Why worry,
it will probably never happen." The words
stamped indelibly upon his subconscious mind
a firm conviction that only good could come into
his life, therefore only good could manifest.

Many a genius has struggled for years with
the problem of supply, when his spoken Word and
faith would have quickly released, needed funds.

After class, one day, a man came to me and
handed me a penny and said, "I have just seven
cents in the world, and I'm going to give you
one; for I have faith in the power of your spoken
Word. I want you to speak the Word for my perfect self-expression and prosperity."

After I "spoke the Word" I didn't see him for a year until he came in one day, successful and happy. He said, "Immediately after you spoke the Word, I had a position offered me in a distant city, and am now demonstrating health, happiness and supply."

A friend was terrified to walk under a ladder. I said, "If you are afraid, you are giving in to a belief in two powers—Good and Evil. To show you believe in only One Power—God, and that there is no power in evil, walk under the next ladder you see."

Later when she went to her bank there stood a ladder on her pathway. Quaking with fear, she turned back because she could not face the lion on her pathway.

When she reached the street, my words rang in her ears and she went back to walk under the ladder. It was a big moment in her life, for ladders had held her in bondage for years. But the ladder was no longer there—as so often happens.

Fear attracted the ladder to her pathway and fearlessness removed it. You can vanquish fear by walking up to the thing you fear.

*Face a situation fearlessly
and it falls away.*

36

Spiritual Secret

Fear must be transmuted into Faith.

❧❧❧

There is no peace or happiness until fear is erased from the subconscious.

The lion takes its fierceness from your fear. Walk up to the lion, and he will disappear; run away from fear and he runs after you. The lion of lack disappears when you spent money fearlessly, showing faith that God is your supply and therefore, unfailing.

> *"Perfect love casteth out fear. He that feareth is not made perfect in love,"* (1 John 4:18)

We have so long separated ourselves from God's good and supply, through thoughts of separation and lack, that sometimes, it takes dynamite to dislodge false ideas from the subconscious. The dynamite is a big situation.

The subconscious is impressed with the Truth that God is the Giver and Gift. As you are one with the Giver, you are one with the Gift.

Affirmation

I thank God, the Giver, for God, the Gift.

Fear is inverted faith,
belief in two powers, good and evil.
There is only one power, God.

Many think that good mothering requires that she worry about her children. But mother-fear is responsible for many diseases and accidents that come into the lives of children due to manifesting her fear-pictures. Happy is the mother who puts her children in God's hands, knowing they are divinely protected.

A woman awoke suddenly, in the night, feeling her brother was in great danger. Instead of giving in to her fears, she commenced making statements of Truth, saying, "Man is a perfect idea in Divine Mind, and is always in his right place, therefore, my brother is in his right place, and is divinely protected."

The next day she found that her brother had been in close proximity to an explosion in a mine, but had miraculously escaped.

Transmute fear into faith by casting
the burden, and putting it
into God's hands.

Soul Sleep

Evil is a false law we have made for ourselves through Soul Sleep.

*False words are not only evil in themselves,
but they infect the soul with evil.*
— Socrates
Plato's Phædo, 91

Soul sleep—being hypnotized by belief in sin, sickness and death—is carnal or mortal thought of the conscious mind. Our affairs are out-pictures of our illusions.

"Resist not evil."
(Matthew 5:39)

Jesus taught that there is no evil, therefore nothing to resist. Evil comes of our "vain imagination," or a belief in two powers, good and evil.

In the Garden of Eden, Adam and Eve ate of "Maya, the Tree of Illusion," and saw two powers instead of one power—God.

God is absolute—there can be no opposing power, unless you make a false law of evil.

**Resistance is Hell, for it places you
in a "state of torment."**

37

Spiritual Secret

Faith is an effort of the Will.

∾❧∾❧∾

It is easier to have fear than faith.

It is, indeed, an effort of the Will to leave the husks and swine of mortal thinking. It is so much easier, for the average person, to have fear than faith; so faith is an effort of the will.

You must substitute faith for fear, for fear and worry are inverted faith. Fear is faith in evil instead of good and through distorted mental pictures, fear brings to pass the thing you fear.

"Why are ye fearful, oh ye of little faith?" (Matthew 8:26)

Your work is to drive out these enemies from your subconscious mind. "When Man is fearless he is finished!" Maeterlinck says, that "Man is God afraid."

Affirmation

I erase fear—fear of lack, fear of failure, fear of sickness, fear of loss—feelings of insecurity—from my consciousness.

"All things are possible to him that believeth." (Mark 9:23)

38

Spiritual Secret

**Your only enemies are
within you.**

❧

**Overcome enemies within and
there no enemies on the external.**

Fear may stand between you and your perfect
self-expression. Indecision may be a stum-
bling-block in your path.

Decision Affirmation

I am always under direct inspiration;
I make right decisions, quickly.

These words impress the subconscious, so you
soon find yourself awake and alert, making right
moves without hesitation.

Stage-fright that has hampered many a
genius can be overcome by the spoken Word.
Shedding self-consciousness you can feel like a
channel for Infinite Intelligence's expression. It
is the "God within" who does the work.

> *"And a man's foes shall be they of
> his own house-hold."* (Psalms 27:8)

Perhaps a habit of incompletion is delaying your demonstration. Give thanks that you have already received on the invisible plane, and make active preparation for receiving on the visible.

A student in need of a financial demonstration asked why it was not completed. I replied: "Perhaps, you are in the habit of leaving things unfinished, and the subconscious has gotten into the habit of not completing— as the without, so the within."

She said, "You are right. I often begin things and never finish them. I'll go home and finish something I commenced weeks ago, and I know it will be symbolic of my demonstration."

So she sewed assiduously and the dress she had previously left unfinished was soon completed. Shortly after, the money came in a most curious manner. Her husband was paid his salary twice that month. He told the people of their mistake, and they sent word for him to keep it.

Completion Demand

In Divine Mind there is only completion, therefore, my demonstration is completed. My perfect work, my perfect home, my perfect health.

39

Spiritual Secret
No one is your enemy, no one is your friend, every one is your teacher.

~~~

Perfect yourself on your neighbor.

A woman was distressed because the man she loved, called Cap, had left her for another woman. She was torn with jealousy and resentment and said she hoped he would suffer as he had made her suffer.

"You are not loving that man, you are hating him," I said and added, "You can never receive what you have never given. Give a perfect love and you will receive a perfect love. Perfect yourself on this man. Give him a perfect, unselfish love, demanding nothing in return. Do not criticize or condemn, and bless him wherever he is."

"No, I won't bless him unless I know where he is!" she said. "That is not real love," I said. "send out real love, real love will return to you, either from this man or his equivalent, for if this man is not the Divine selection, you will not want him. As you are one with God, you are one with the love which belongs to you by Divine Right."

I said, "When his cruelty no longer disturbs you, he will cease to be cruel, as you are attracting it through your obsessing over him."

I told her of a brotherhood in India, who never said, "Good Morning" to each other. They used these words: "I salute the Divinity in you." They saluted the Divinity in every man, and in the wild animals in the jungle, and they were never harmed, for they saw only God in every living thing.

I said, "Salute the Divinity in this man, and say, 'I see your Divine Self only. I see you as God sees you, perfect, made in His image and likeness.'"

She became more poised, and gradually lost her resentment. One day, she said, suddenly, "God bless Cap wherever he is."

I replied: "Now that is real love, and when you have become a 'complete circle,' and are no longer disturbed by the situation, you will have his love, or attract its equivalent."

A while later I received a letter saying, "We are married." I called her and asked, "What happened?" "Oh," she exclaimed, "a miracle! One day I woke up and all suffering had ceased. I saw Cap that evening and he asked me to marry him. We were married in about a week, and I have never seen a more devoted man."

The lover was teaching her selfless love, which we all, sooner or later, must learn.

―――

40

Spiritual Secret
Bless a man and he has no
power to harm you.

❧⌘❧

Send goodwill to others.

A man came to me asking to "treat" for success in business. He was selling machinery and a rival appeared on the scene with what he proclaimed was a better machine. My friend feared defeat.

I said, "Don't hold one critical thought towards that man. Bless him all day, and be willing to not sell your machine, if it isn't the Divine Idea. Wipe out all fear, and know that God protects your interests, and that the Divine Idea must come out of the situation. Trust that the right machine will be sold, by the right man, to the right man."

He went to the meeting, fearless and nonresistant, and blessing the other man. He sold his product without the slightest difficulty because the other man's machine refused to work.

"But I say unto you, love your enemies, bless them that curse you, do good to them that hate you, and pray for them which despitefully use you and persecute you." (Mathew 5"44)

41

Spiritual Secret

Go with the flow.

Use the Law of Nonresistance.

The Chinese say that water is the most powerful element, because it is perfectly nonresistant. Water does not resist, it flows around, under and over obstacles. Yet, it wears away rocks, cuts through mountains, and sweeps away all before it.

Watch Water Flow

Go into your yard, turn on a faucet and allow water to run through a hose. Notice where and how the water travels. It flows toward the lowest point. When an object is in its path, the water will flow around it.

Tiny steams of water follow the path of least resistance to form streams, then rivers to flow ultimately into the ocean. While the water flows around every object in its path, it makes changes to all it flows over and around.

42

Spiritual Secret

What you resist, persists.

**Resisting a situation leaves you
with little energy to overcome it.**

When you resist a situation, you obsess over it thereby empowering and strengthening it, so that it affects you more negatively.

Stop resisting. Let go and allow.

Letting go releases an enormous amount of energy that is holding that resistance or block in place. You free up that energy when you allow.

Affirmation

It is okay to be afraid to let go of _____. I deeply and completely love and accept myself and I choose to be open to surrendering _____. I choose to feel safe and to be there for me, I am okay and completely safe".

*"Resist not evil. Be not overcome
of evil, but overcome evil with
good."* (Romans 12:21)

A woman was afraid because her daughter was planning hazardous trip. Pointing out the dangers, she forbid her to go, but the daughter was determined. I said to the woman, "You are forcing your personal will upon your daughter, which you have no right to do. Your fear of the trip is attracting it because you attract what you fear."

"Let go. Take your mental hands off your daughter. Put it in God's Hands. Use this statement:

> "I put this situation in the hands of Infinite Love and Wisdom; if this trip is the Divine plan, I bless it and no longer resist, but if it is not divinely planned, I give thanks that it is now dissolved and dissipated."

A day or two after that, her daughter told her, "Mother, I have given up the trip," and the situation returned to its "native nothingness."

> *"Stand ye still and see the salvation of the Lord (Law)."*
> (2 Chronicles 20:17)

43

Spiritual Secret

What you condemn in others, you attract to yourself.

This is the Law of Attraction.

You attract disease and unhappiness by condemning others.

> *Condemn not lest ye also be condemned."* (Luke 6:37)

"A friend was angry because her husband deserted her for another woman. Condemning the other woman, she said continually, "She knew he was a married man, and had no right to accept his attentions."

I replied: "Stop condemning the woman, bless her, and be through with the situation, otherwise, you are attracting the same thing to yourself."

She was deaf to my words, and a year or two later, became deeply interested in a married man, herself.

You pick up a live-wire whenever you condemn; so expect a shock.

How to Recognize
an Internal Battle

Notice the thoughts going through your
mind when you are resisting your current
challenge or situation.

> *"I hate my life."*
> *"I can never do anything right."*
> *"Nobody likes me."*
> *"I'm to fat, to ugly, to stupid…"*

These are negative, disempowering thoughts,
words you say to yourself that take you further
from your dreams.

Write down your negative "self-talk" in a
notebook. Then rewrite each statement to be
positive. When you catch yourself talking negatively to yourself, yell "Stop!" in your mind, and
switch to telling yourself the positive statement.

> *"Life is good."*
> *"I have many skills."*
> *"I am likeable."*
> *"I am healthy and strong."*

The more you do this practice, the easier it is to
catch and rewrite your negative self-talk.

44

Spiritual Secret

Struggle results from going upstream.

Struggle is the first sign of resistance.

Struggling with problems that cannot be solved indicate you are going against, rather than with the Flow of Life.

Change direction when you notice that you keep struggling with a particular situation. When something constantly prevents you from overcoming an obstacle, identify your options for a different approach instead of continuing to struggle with the situation.

Life is a series of natural and spontaneous changes. Don't resist them – that only creates sorrow. Let reality be reality. Let things flow naturally forward in whatever way they like.

—Lao-Tzu

When you catch yourself in an internal battle, struggling with a challenge, notice how you are going against the natural flow of life. Change direction. Do the opposite. Replace negative thoughts with positive ones. Take action that is aligned with positive thoughts to break the chain of resistance.

45

Spiritual Secret

Surrender.

∞◦⌘◦∞

Anxiety and fear is resistance in disguise.

To those who worry, "I don't want to be a doormat" I reply, "when you use nonresistance with wisdom, no one will ever be able to walk on you."

One day I was impatiently awaiting an important telephone call. I refused every call that came in and made no out-going calls, worrying that I might miss the call I was awaiting.

Instead of saying, "Divine Ideas never conflict, the call will come at the right time," and leaving it to Infinite Intelligence to arrange, I commenced to try to manage things myself. I made the battle mine, not God's, remaining tense and anxious. When the phone did not ring for over an hour, I sensed something was wrong and found it was unplugged.

My anxiety, fear, and belief in interference had brought on a total eclipse of the telephone.

"Oh Judah, fear not;
but tomorrow go out against them,

for the Lord will be with you.
You shall not need to fight this battle;
set yourselves, stand ye still,
and see the salvation
of the Lord with you."
(2 Chronicles 20:17)

Realizing what I had done, I blessed the situation. I baptized it "success" and affirmed, "I cannot lose any call that belongs to me by Divine Right. I am under Grace, and not under Law."

I plugged the phone and two minutes later, I received a very important call I'd not been expecting, and about an hour afterwards, the call I had been awaiting came in.

Affirmation

My ship comes in over a calm sea.

Letting go sounds like you will lose control. You are in control when you allow. Allow yourself to relax. Allow yourself to agree with your adversary. Surrender.

I will restore to you the years
the locusts have eaten."
(Joel 2:25)

The locusts are the doubts, fears, resentments and regrets of mortal thinking. These adverse thoughts, alone, rob you.

46

Spiritual Secret

Accept difficulties.

Use the Law of Nonresistance.

Never fight difficulties you encounter. Instead, accept them, surrender to them. When you give out positive energy, positive energy comes back. When you take a positive action to solve a problem, you will get a solved problem in return. Use the Law of Nonresistance: always take positive rather than negative action. Don't crash though obstacles, flow around them.

Stress and the pressures of life are released through surrender.

"Letting go" is one of the most healthy things you can do. It leads to an inner peace, a release of pressure, a new freedom. "Letting go" ultimately leads to a peace and freedom beyond anything that you or I have yet experienced.

47

Spiritual Secret

**As long as you resist a situation,
it stays with you.**

∽∾⌒∾⌒∾

**Inharmonious situations come from
inharmony within ourselves.**

If you run away from an inharmonious situation, it will run after you. When you make no emotional response, it fades away forever from your pathway.

When I explained this Spiritual Secret to a woman, she replied, "How true that is! I was unhappy at home, I disliked my mother, who was critical and domineering; so I ran away and was married—but I married my mother, for my husband was exactly like her. I had the same situation to face again."

*"Agree with thine adversary
quickly."* (Matthew 5:25)

Do not resist. Instead, agree that the adverse situation is good, be undisturbed by it, and it falls away of its own weight.

Affirmation
None of these things move me.

48

Spiritual Secret

Live fully in the Now.

~~~~

The past and the future rob your time.

You must live suspended in the moment. Bless the past and forget it. Bless the future, knowing it has endless joys in store for you, then live fully in the *Now*.

> *"Behold, now is the accepted time. Now is the day of Salvation."* (2 Corinthians 6:2)

A woman with no money to buy Christmas gifts, said, "Last year I had plenty of money and gave lovely presents. This year I have scarcely a cent." I reminded her, "You will never demonstrate money while you are pathetic and live in the past. Live fully in the Now and get ready to give Christmas presents. Dig your ditches and the money will come."

"I know what to do!" she exclaimed. "I will buy tinsel twine, Christmas seals and wrapping paper." I replied, "Do that, and the presents will come and stick themselves to the Christmas seals."

She showed financial fearlessness and faith in God; whereas the reasoning mind says, "Keep every cent as you are not sure you will get any more."

The woman bought the seals, paper and twine. A few days before Christmas, she received a gift of several hundred dollars. Buying the seals and twine had impressed the subconscious with expectancy and opened the way for the manifestation of the money. She purchased all the presents for her loved ones in plenty of time.

Salutation to the Dawn

Look to this day!
For it is life, the very life of life.
In its brief course
Lie all the verities and realities
of your existence:
The bliss of growth
The glory of action
The splendor of beauty
For yesterday is but a dream
And tomorrow only a vision
But today well lived makes every yester-
day a dream of happiness
And every tomorrow a vision of hope.
Look well, therefore to this day!
Such is the salutation to the dawn.

—Kalidasa, Indian Poet

Lot's wife looked back
and turned into a pillar of salt.

49

Spiritual Secret
Cast the Burden

A burden is an adverse thought or condition with roots in the subconscious.

A metaphysician explained it like this. "The only thing which gives anything weight in nature is the Law of Gravitation, and if a boulder could be taken high above the planet, there would be no weight in that boulder. That is what Jesus meant when he said: 'My yoke is easy and my burden is light.'" He had overcome the world vibration, and functioned in the fourth dimensional realm, where there is only perfection, completion, life and joy.

> *"Come to me all ye that labor and are heavy laden, and I will give you rest... Take my yoke upon you, for my yoke is easy and my burden is light."* (Matthew 11:28-30)

The fifty-fifth Psalm says to "cast thy burden upon the Lord." Many passages in *The Bible* say the "battle is God's" not ours and that we should "stand still", or surrender, and accept the Salvation of the Lord.

The superconscious mind—God within—is the department that fights our battles and relieves us of burdens.

"The Christ in you, the hope of glory." (Colossian 1:27)

It's almost impossible to make any headway by trying to direct the subconscious with the reasoning mind, as the reasoning mind—the intellect—is limited in its conceptions, and filled with doubts and fears.

An intellectual knowledge of the Truth alone will not bring results.

Instead, cast your burden upon the superconscious mind—God within—where it will be "made light" and dissolve into its "native nothingness."

Affirmation
I cast this burden on the Christ within,
and go free.

Cast the Burden

A woman in urgent need of money, said, "I cast this burden of lack on the God within and I go free to have plenty!" The belief in lack was her burden, and as she cast it upon the God within, the superconscious flooded the subconscious with its belief of plenty and an avalanche of supply was the result.

A student had been given a new piano but there was no room in her studio until she moved the old piano out, but she wanted to keep it. She was desperate because the new piano was on its way, with no place to put it. She repeated, "I cast this burden on the God within, and I go free." A few moments later, her phone rang and a friend asked if she might rent her old piano. It was moved out, a few minutes before the new one arrived.

A woman was burdened with resentment. She said, "I cast this burden of resentment on the God within, and I go free, to be loving, harmonious and happy." The Almighty superconscious flooded the subconscious with love, and her whole life changed. For years, resentment had held her in a state of torment and imprisoned her soul—subconscious mind.

The statement should be made repeatedly, for hours at a time, silently or audibly, with quietness but determination. Like winding up a Victrola, wind yourself up with the spoken Word.

In steadily repeating the affirmation

> "I cast this burden on the Christ within,
> and go free."

the vision clears, and with it a feeling of relief, and sooner or later comes the manifestation of good, be it health, happiness or supply.

It is impossible to have clear vision while in the throes of reasoning mind. Doubts and fear poison the mind and body and the imagination runs riot, attracting disaster and disease.

Darkest Before the Dawn

A big demonstration is usually preceded by tormenting thoughts. Deep depression clouds consciousness with rising fears and doubts. Everything seems to go wrong. This is the darkness before dawn when old derelicts (worries) of the subconscious rise to the surface, to be put out.

This is the moment to clap your cymbals, like Jehoshaphat, and give thanks that you are saved, even though seemingly surrounded by the enemy—the situation of lack or disease.

A student asked, "How long must one remain in the dark" and I replied, "until you can see in the dark. Until you can create an image of good, believe in it, and hold to it with active faith.

Demonstrations often come at the 11th hour,
as the reasoning mind lets go
—surrenders—
so Infinite Intelligence can work.

50

Spiritual Secret
What you send out
returns to you.

∽≈≪≫≈∽

This is Karmic Law.

Your thoughts, deeds and words return to you with astounding accuracy.

If you give hate, you will receive hate;

If you give love, you will receive love;

If you give criticism, you will receive criticism;

If you lie, you will be lied to;

If you cheat, you will be cheated.

If you are kind, you will receive kindness
—sooner or later.

The Karmic clock does not follow human time. What goes around comes around.

*The Game of Life is
a game of boomerangs.*

What you seek
is seeking you.

Spiritual Secret

Suffering results from violating Spiritual Law.

Suffering is not necessary for your development.

When people are happy, they may become selfish so that the Law of Karma is set in action. Many suffer loss through lack of appreciation.

A woman with a nice husband said often, "I don't care anything about being married, but that is nothing against my husband. I'm simply not interested in married life."

She had other interests, and only thought of him when she saw him. One day her husband told her he was in love with another woman, and left. She was filled with resentment.

I replied, "It is exactly what you spoke the Word for. You said you didn't care anything about being married, so the subconscious worked to get you unmarried."

She said, "Oh yes, I see. People get what they want, and then feel very much hurt."

52

Spiritual Secret

Plenty is always on your path.

∽∾∾∽

Break down barriers of lack in your consciousness and the Golden Age will be yours.

You prosper in direct proportion to your enjoyment in seeing it for others; while prosperity is denied in proportion to your feelings of guilt for being prosperous, or at the envy and hostility you feel about other's prosperity.

> *"Yea, the Almighty shall be thy defense and thou shalt have plenty of silver."* (Job 22:25)

If you think, feel, act and speak of yourself as being poor and needy you must spend three times the energy for the same prosperity received by those who think, feel, act, and speak of themselves as being wealthy and prosperous.

> *Abundance is not something we acquire. It is something we tune into.*
> —Dr. Wayne Dyer

God's design is for your barn to be full and your cup to flow over with plenty.

Affirmation

Having plenty is my Divine Right.

53

Spiritual Secret

Wealth is a matter of consciousness.

It is your consciousness of gold, of opulence, that brings riches into your life.

According to a French legend a poor man was walking along a road when he met a traveler, who said: "My good friend, I see you are poor; take this gold nugget, sell it, and you will be rich all your days."

Overjoyed at his good fortune, he took the nugget home. He immediately found work and became so prosperous that he did not sell the nugget. Years passed, and he became a very rich man. One day he met a poor man on the road. He stopped him and said: "My good friend, I will give you this gold nugget, which, if you sell, will make you rich for life." The man took the nugget, had it valued, and found it was only brass.

So we see, the first man became rich through feeling rich, thinking the nugget was gold; the second man had no faith and stayed poor.

Affirmation

I have a gold nugget within myself.

54

Spiritual Secret

Money is God in manifestation.

❧~❧

The great Bank of the Universe never fails.

Money brings freedom from want and limitation, so long as it is kept in circulation and put to right uses. Hoarding and saving react with grim vengeance.

This does not mean that you should not have houses and lots, stocks and bonds, for the barns of the righteous shall be full; it means you should not hoard even the principal, if an occasion arises, when money is necessary. In letting it go fearlessly and cheerfully, you open the way for more to come in, for God is your unfailing and inexhaustible supply.

A woman won five thousand dollars in a lottery, but would not spend it. She hoarded and saved, let her husband suffer and starve, and eventually she scrubbed floors for a living.

She loved the money itself and put it above everything, and one night she was murdered and the money taken from her. This is an example of where "love of money is the root of all evil."

~

Spiritual Secret

**You cannot attract money if
you despise it.**

~

**You must be in harmony with money
to attract it.**

Many people are kept in poverty by saying:
"Money means nothing to me, and I have
a contempt for people who have it."

Many artists are poor because their contempt
for money separates them from it.

I remember hearing one artist say of another,
"He's no good as an artist, he has money in the
bank."

This attitude of mind, of course, separates
you from your supply; you must be in harmony
with a thing in order to attract it.

Prosperity Affirmation

God is my unfailing supply. Large sums
of money come to me quickly,
under grace, in perfect way.

Spiritual Secret

**Gifts are investments;
hoarding leads to loss.**

❧❧

**The Law stands back of the man who spends
fearlessly, with wisdom.**

If you ignore leads to spend or to give, the
same amount of money will go out in an unin-
teresting or unhappy way.

A woman informed her family that they
could not afford a Thanksgiving dinner. She had
the money, but decided to save it. A few days
later, someone entered her room and took from
the bureau drawer the exact amount that the
dinner would have cost.

A student was shopping with her little neph-
ew. The child clamored for a toy, which she told
him she could not afford to buy. She realized suddenly that she was seeking lack and not recog-
nizing God as her supply! So she bought the toy,
and on her way home, picked up on the street the
exact amount of money she had paid for the toy.

Spiritual Secret

**Act as if you have already received
what you demand.**

∽౸✑∾✑౸∽

**God is your supply
There is a supply for every demand.**

A friend was in great distress because she was
to be sued for several thousand dollars on
the fifteenth of the month and she knew no way
of getting the money.

So I spoke the Word! "I gave thanks that my
friend would receive the money needed, at the
right time, in the right way, provided she had
perfect faith and acted according to perfect faith."
The fifteenth came but no money had material-
ized.

My friend was worried. I reminded her, "It
is Saturday. They can't sue you on a weekend.
Act rich to show your perfect faith that you will
receive the money you need by Monday." We
met for lunch to keep up her courage. When
ordering our meal, I said, "This is no time to
economize. Act as if you have already received
the needed money." I reminded her. "You are
divinely protected and God is never too late."

She called the next day greatly excited, "My dear, a miracle has happened! I was sitting in my room this morning, when the doorbell rang. It was my wealthy cousin who I'd not seen in a long while. We visited for about an hour, and just as he was leaving, he asked, 'These are hard times. How are finances?' I told him I needed the money, and he quickly replied, 'Why, my dear, I will give you the money you need on the first of the month.'"

"I didn't want to tell him about the suit. I won't receive the money till the first of the month, and I must have it tomorrow. What should I do?" she implored. "I'll keep on 'treating,'" I replied.

I said, "Spirit is never too late. I give thanks my friend has received the money on the invisible plane and that it manifests on time." The next morning my friend's cousin called, "Come to my office this morning to pick up the check." That afternoon, my friend had enough money in her account to pay off her debt, and wrote the check as rapidly as her excitement would permit.

Make your affirmations of truth repeatedly and rejoice and give thanks that you've <u>already received</u> what you seek.

58

Spiritual Secret

You get the situation for which you have prepared.

◦◦◦◦◦

Prepare to receive what you have demanded—even if it seems unlikely.

There is a wonderful illustration in *The Bible* of three kings stranded in the desert, without water for their men and horses. The kings consulted the prophet Elisha, who gave them an astonishing message:

> *"Thus saith the Lord—Ye shall not see wind, neither shall ye see rain, yet make this valley full of ditches."*
> (2 Kings 3:17)

A man asked me to speak the Word that a debt would be wiped out. He should have been picturing himself paying off his debt but he spent his time planning what he would say when he did not pay his bill—thereby neutralizing my words.

> *"The ditches dug by the three kings in the desert were filled to overflowing."* (2 Kings)

A woman had to move to a new apartment at a time when there was a great shortage of apartments in New York. Finding a decent apartment was considered almost an impossibility. Friends consoled her, "It's too bad you'll have live in a hotel and store your furniture." She replied, "Don't feel sorry for me. I have faith that I will find a good apartment to rent.

She knew there was a supply for every demand so spoke the words many times a day:

"Infinite Spirit, open the way for the right apartment." The woman knew she was "unconditioned," working on the spiritual plane, and that "one with God is a majority."

She contemplated buying a new rug for the apartment, "the tempter"—adverse thought of the reasoning mind—warned, "Don't buy the rug because you probably won't find an apartment and will have no use for it." Catching her negativity, she promptly replied silently to herself: "I'll dig my ditches by buying the rug!" The woman acted as if she already had a new apartment by buying the rug, which showed her faith.

A short time later the woman found an exceptional apartment in a miraculous way even though there were over two hundred other applicants. Buying the rug showed active faith.

Your supply is inexhaustible.

59

Spiritual Secret

**Giving opens the way
for receiving.**

~⊙~⊙~

To create activity in finances, you must give.

Tithing—giving one-tenth of your income—is an old Jewish custom, and is sure to bring increase. Many of the richest men in this country have been tithers. I have never known it to fail as an investment.

The tenth-part goes forth and returns blessed and multiplied. But the gift or tithe must be given with love and cheerfulness.

"God loveth a cheerful giver."
(2 Corinthians 9:7)

Send all money forth fearlessly and with a blessing. Pay bills cheerfully. This attitude of mind makes you master of money. Money is yours to obey, and your spoken Word opens vast reservoirs of wealth.

*You, yourself, limit your supply
by your limited vision.*

A woman asked me to "speak the Word" for a position. So I demanded:

> "Infinite Spirit, open the way for this woman's right position."

Never ask for just "a position"; ask for the right position, the place already planned in Divine Mind, as it is the only one that will get satisfaction.

I then gave thanks that she had already received, and that it would manifest quickly. Very soon, she had three positions offered her, two in New York and one in Palm Beach, and she did not know which to choose. I said, "Ask for a definite lead."

She was still undecided, when she woke up one morning and could smell Palm Beach." She had been there before and knew its balmy fragrance.

I told her: "Well, if you can smell Palm Beach from here, it is certainly your lead." She accepted the position, and it proved a great success.

60

Spiritual Secret

Receive gracefully.

**Accept the bread returning
to you upon the water.**

Some people are cheerful givers, but bad receivers. They refuse gifts through pride, or some negative reason, thereby blocking their channels, and invariably find themselves eventually with little or nothing.

A woman who had given away a great deal of money, refused a gift of several thousand dollars, saying she did not need it. Shortly after that, her finances were "tied up," and she found herself in debt for that amount.

> *"Freely ye have given, freely ye shall receive."* (Matthew 10:8)

There is a perfect balance of giving and receiving. While you should give without thinking of returns, you violate Law if you do not accept the returns that come to you; for all gifts are from God, you being merely the channel.

**A thought of lack
should never be held over the giver.**

When the man gave me the one penny, I did not say: "Poor man, he cannot afford to give me that." I saw him rich and prosperous, with his supply pouring in. It was this thought which brought it.

> *The Lord loveth a cheerful receiver, as well as a cheerful giver.* (2 Corinthians 9:7)

If you have been a bad receiver, you must become a good one, and take even a postage stamp if it is given to you, and open up your channels for receiving.

61

Spiritual Secret

Demand that the
Will of God be done.

୬ଚ୬୰

Believe. Have faith.

The secret to winning at the Game of Life is to replace mental pictures of evil by impressing your subconscious mind with a realization of good. Instead of worrying, expect a miracle.

Affirmation

Every false prophecy shall come to naught;
every plan my Father in heaven has not
planned, shall be dissolved and dissipated,
the Divine Idea now comes to pass.

The Law of Expectancy says that when you get a good message of coming happiness, or wealth, if you harbor and expect it, it will manifest—sooner or later.

No man gives to himself but himself,
and no man takes away from himself,
but himself.

62

Spiritual Secret

Your Soul and Spirit
seek to be one.

**Soul is the subconscious and
Spirit is the superconscious.**

The "mystical marriage" is the marriage of the soul and the spirit, or the subconscious and superconscious minds. They must be one. When the subconscious is flooded with the perfect ideas of the superconscious, God and man are one.

> *"I and the Father are one."*
> (John 10:30)

Sacred Marriage

When you make the two into one, and when you make the inner like the outer and the outer like the inner, and the upper like the lower, and when you make male and female into a single one, so that the male will not be male nor the female be female, when you make eyes in place of an eye, a hand in place of a hand, a foot in place of a foot, an image in place of an image, then you will enter the Kingdom.

—Gospel of Thomas, 22

Overcoming the Last Enemy

World thought is that of sin, sickness and death. Jesus saw their absolute unreality and said sickness and sorrow shall pass away and death itself, the last enemy, be overcome.

Christianity is founded upon the forgiveness of sins and "an empty tomb." You will no longer throw off your body in death, but will be would be transformed into the "body electric".

Working under the direction of the superconscious—God within you—the "resurrection of the body" will be accomplished.

I Sing the Body Electric
By Walt Whitman

I sing the body electric,

The armies of those I love engirth me
and I engirth them,

They will not let me off till I go with
them, respond to them,

And discorrupt them, and charge them
full with the charge of the soul.

Was it doubted that those who corrupt
their own bodies conceal themselves?

And if those who defile the living
are as bad as they who defile the dead?

And if the body does not do fully
as much as the soul?

And if the body were not the soul,
what is the soul?

Think as An Artist

Make an art of thinking in pictures—imaging. Be careful to paint only the Divine
Designs upon the canvas of your mind.
Paint your pictures with masterly strokes
of power and decision, having perfect
faith that there is no power to mar their
perfection, and that they shall manifest in
your life, the ideal made real.

Goal of the Game of Life

All power is given you through right thinking to bring your Heaven upon earth, and this is the goal of the "Game of Life."

Rules

The simple rules are fearless faith, nonresistance and love!

Use your Will to hold the perfect vision, without wavering.

Givens

It is God's will to give you every righteous desire of your heart.

Whatever you demand are perfect ideas registered in Divine Mind, and must manifest, "under grace in a perfect way.

Challenge

Your work is in making yourself <u>believe</u> that "with God all things are possible."

The Truth Shall Set You Free

May you be now freed from that thing which has held you in bondage through the ages, standing between you and your own, and "know the Truth shall make you free"—free to fulfill your destiny, to bring into manifestation the "Divine Design of your life, Health, Wealth, Love and Perfect Self-Expression."

Through the Truth, you are set free from the Law of Karma, sin and death. Freedom comes through fulfilling your destiny, bringing into manifestation the Divine Design of your life.

The Universe
rearranges itself
to bring you
what you believe.

"with God all things are possible."
(Matthew 19:26)

Florence Scovel Shinn was a popular New Thought teacher and author in the early 20th Century—and still has an international following. Born in Camden, New Jersey in 1871 into a well-to-do family, Shinn studied art at the Pennsylvania Academy of Fine Arts where she met her husband, Everett Shinn, a celebrated impressionistic painter. While Shinn started off her career illustrating popular children's magazines and books, after WWI she began writing inspirational New Thought books.

Having taught metaphysics in New York for many years, Shinn had the ability to bring metaphysical ideas down to earth for everyday people. She explained spiritual principles in an entertaining and easy style.

She shows how positive attitudes and affirmations succeed in making one a "winner" in life — able to control life's conditions and release abundance through a knowledge of spiritual law. By applying spiritual laws we can enjoy good health, prosperity, and happiness.

Affirmations are at the center of Shinn's method, which continue to circulate in the New Thought literature today. Her wisdom appeals to readers who want guidance in difficult times. Shinn never sought to be literary, conventional, or impressive, which appealed to the thousands who read her Works. She was always herself — colloquial, informal, friendly, and humorous.

Dr. **Beverly Potter** earned her Masters of Science in vocational rehabilitation counseling from San Francisco State and her Doctorate in counseling psychology from Stanford University. She has authored several books about workplace issues that blend the philosophies of humanistic psychology and Eastern mysticism with principles of behavior psychology.

Spiritual Secrets was derived from Florence Scovel Shinn's loved classic, *The Game of Life & How to Play It*, which is in the public domain. This is a total transformation, to create a wholly new book, in Shinn's words, with her endearing stories. Docpotter used her unique style of "repurposing", as some have called it, to take out of print books by Timothy Leary to create ten fresh new books, including *Your Brain is God* and *Start Your Own Religion*. In a similar manner, she also created three new books by John C. Lilly, M.D., including *Programming the Human BioComputer* and *The Quiet Center*. She likens the process to a kind of channeling.

A scene from *Gone with the Wind* is Docpotter's metaphor these derivitative works. Scarlet wanted to get Rhet back, but didn't want him to know she was poor and desperate. She needed to look rich and pampered. Looking around Tara she saw the beautiful red velvet drapes, which she cut up to create a stunning red velvet gown, fit for a queen. Docpotter takes the velvet of old classics to create new Works.

Her website is *docpotter.com*. You can also find Docpotter on Twitter, Facebook and elsewhere in cyberspace and the cloud. Please visit.

Books by Beverly Potter

Beyond Conscious
What Happens After Death

Overcoming Job Burnout
How to Renew Enthusiasm for Work

The Worrywart's Companion
Twenty-One Ways to Soothe Yourself & Worry Smart

From Conflict to Cooperation
How to Mediate a Dispute

Finding a Path with a Heart
How to Go from Burnout to Bliss

Preventing Job Burnout
A Workbook

The Way of the Ronin
Riding the Waves of Change at Work

High Performance Goal Setting
Using Intuition to Conceive & Achieve Your Dreams

Brain Boosters
Foods & Drugs that Make You Smarter

Drug Testing at Work
A Guide for Employers

Pass the Test
An Employee's Guide to Drug Testing

The Healing Magic of Cannabis
It's the High that Heals

Turning Around
Keys to Motivation and Productivity

Bless you,
Florence.